Coffee Cat

Puróy Manálo

Ukiyoto Publishing

All global publishing rights are held by

Ukiyoto Publishing

Published in 2024

Content Copyright © Puróy Manálo

ISBN 9789362696243

All rights reserved.
No part of this publication may be reproduced, transmitted, or stored in a retrieval system, in any form by any means, electronic, mechanical, photocopying, recording or otherwise, without the prior permission of the publisher.

The moral rights of the author have been asserted.

This is a work of fiction. Names, characters, businesses, places, events, locales, and incidents are either the products of the author's imagination or used in a fictitious manner. Any resemblance to actual persons, living or dead, or actual events is purely coincidental.

This book is sold subject to the condition that it shall not by way of trade or otherwise, be lent, resold, hired out or otherwise circulated, without the publisher's prior consent, in any form of binding or cover other than that in which it is published.

www.ukiyoto.com

Dedication

I dedicate this book to my nephew Bótchok del Pilar, to Mía Mae, to Kuya Ariel Merjúdio and family, to Peter Paul Phils., and to my former boss CCT MPC.

Also, I dedicate these poems to all Malvareños, Pagbilaoins and Catánauanins.

Introduction

"With me poetry has not been a purpose, but a passion."
EDGAR ALLAN POE

"Poetry comes nearer to vital truth than history."
PLATO

Poetry is not an end in itself. Poetry is a vessel of truth initiated by our Primordial Author.

All literature began with "the Word" (Λόγος), when God created the world (and everything in it). Literature wasn't meant to be, and shouldn't be, a Tower of Babel. Literature isn't supposed to be in competition with the Word, nor meant to be an improvement of all Creation.

It is a light and lens for us to see what's already existent. Poetry makes us see, feel, and hear the truth that was already there when the Cosmos came into being by His Word.

We read about the truth, but we feel it through Poetry— we immerse our souls in its very essence.

These books are among my various contributions for the World in its quest for the Truth.

Soli Deo Gloria.

Acknowledgements

There wouldn't have been another book without the help of my peers and closest friends.

I thank my former classmates and professors for the support; my co-workers, and church mates for inspiring me to continue writing. I also thank my former employers for keeping open the doors behind me.

Thank you, Kuya Ariel Merjúdio and family, for welcoming me into your home.

Special thanks to my manager, Boss Red F., for promoting my previous poems. I also thank Jeff Jàvier for the technical advice, and Jolína Lìngao for the design comments.

I thank all those who bought copies of my earlier works. May you keep on patronizing my books.

This sequel of my works wouldn't have been complete without your support. Many thanks to all of you, and to God be all the Glory.

Δόξα τω θεώ.

Synopsis

The author tackles some of life's most pressing issues through poetry. Most of these poems are based on the poet's experience. In this book are advices to the youth, to fellow bachelors, to the fellow middle-aged losers, and to anyone in general. Life is not life without the arts, and poetry and music in particular. It's just existence. This book will help us live the "life" as it should be.

Contents

Fulfillment	1
Forgive the Apple in My Paradise	2
Place Your Order Here	3
Gluten-Free	4
The Cosmic Sonnet	5
Dedication and Acknowledgment	6
About the Author and Blurb	7
Our Next Stop-Over: Planet Earth	8
Thirteenth Month Pay	9
Epitaph	10
Seclusión Perpetua	11
On A Single Night	12
O Calcutta!	13
God Bless America	14
Peace of Mind	15
Robert	16
My Last Last Will to the Poet's Daughter	17
Tantalus	18
My Ex-Face	19
Coffee Cat	20
Way Ahead of Schedule	21
Sincerely Yours, Onésimus	22
In the Book Fair	23
Well Experienced, Now a Poet	24
The Quota and the Deadline	25
Renaissance	26
A Bachelor's Cat	27
"I Googled It"	28
The Prototype	29
The Prescription	30
Continue to Perpetuity	31
The Baccalaureate Guest Speaker	32

Aristotle's Oasis	33
A Dozen Roses in the Scrap Bin	34
For My Protégé	35
Maverick	36
2023 Point 99	37
The Rush	38
Simplicity	39
The Future Is A Book	40
The Empty Pocket	41
The Baccalaureate Guest Speaker 2	42
Poetry	43
Thanatopsis	44
Time	45
The Future	46
Burning on Both Ends	47
Kamag-anak, Inc.	48
Híjo de Ferrócaríl	49
Froilan's Touch	50
Valentine's Day	51
Sóla Grátia	52
The Hopeless Alchemist	53
Practicality	54
Paper Hopes	55
On Paper Ground	56
Regaining Glory	64
About the Author	*65*

Fulfillment

Around the bend I met the younger sunshine,
Reflected on the dewy tendrils of a vine.
Half-open flower buds and tender shoots,
Half-hidden secrets and half-open truths.
The darkness of the night was past behind,
I'll sniff the blossoming daylight that I'll find.
  The dark and trackless trail before the bend,
  To distant, fading memory I send.

The daily grind and listless journey end,
To climb up higher is what I intend.
Before the day grow old to sunset hours,
I'll keep on hiking 'til the zenith's ours.
  The failures of the distant days of old,
  Are now replaced by blissful days of gold.

Forgive the Apple in My Paradise

My love, you are the reddest apple on display,
And I the bluest ogre in the heap of hay.
An apple is a red, red rose, and thus,
An apple is a rose, is a rose … forget the fuss.
The worm invisibly destroys the apple tree,
Nocturnal howling in a crimson spree.
  That shiny, scarlet, juicy crispiness,
  Brought sin— my death— to nip my happiness.

The apples, pears and roses— I can't eat the last—
It's you I yearn for in a holy fast.
Unwitting temptress you have been to me,
You'll burn my soul in the sulphuric sea.
  "Forget the apple pie and seek the cross,
  A better apple can be grown by Bestie Boss."

Place Your Order Here

Thank you for calling Froilan & Sons, Limited,
This is the father speaking, how can I help you?
Huh... huh? uhum, right now...
The truth of the matter is, it doesn't matter if
in cobwebs and dust my works lay untouched
And none buys the lot,
As Goodyear died impoverished, my works
Shall flourish in a later year.
Floránte said that he'll grow old
And pass away,
But his songs he'll leave us
For us to sing.
Van Gogh!
But better still my works as Peter Pan be,
It left a legacy
Worth funding hospitals...
As I was saying, Sir... What? Sorry, Sir, I
Was musing under the influence. The...
O yes... We never fail to deliver, and
If you order ten copies, or
Buy three copies each of my five books, You'll
Get a hefty discount. Then... I beg your pardon?
What! A hundred copy of every title!
O sure! *Un momento*, I'll get a pen...
Okay... okay, a hundred of "Froilan's, Ltd."
The same with "Puróy's Second."
A hundred of...
Si, your address is... Eight, Six,
Six... Seven... Padilla? ... Padilla street... Cebú Ci...

Gluten-Free

Pristine received you this, pristine you preach—
Deceive not apples into peach.
Extenders you'll not find, not chemical coloured,
It should be NÁPA, naturally flavoured.
The life-giving water is purer than distilled,
Keep that to your child's mind instilled.
  Deceived you kosher from your father,
  Pollute it not with fillers any further.

Unleavened bread from heaven is the Word,
In breaking of the bread, you use no Sword.
The Bread, true bromate-free— organic—
Must be consumed in peace, and not in panic.
  Your father fed you healthy drink and food,
  So feed your children life's holistic good.

The Cosmic Sonnet

These poems did not come from Dushanbe,
These came from Pagbiláo, as true can be.
But needed be, from Marrakesh these hail,
So that the blind can read my poems in braille.
Admit with tickets, any colour pass,
Cain's mark or Judgment seal— of any class.
  You see my God is colour-blind, but see
  Through walls, and enter hearts without a key.

I may be brown— or yellow— orange if you must—
A cosmopolitan god created me from dust.
You're not the rightful judge but He alone,
Your senseless voice, it seems, as dry as bone.
  A better critique, these, my works deserve,
  And not some nonsense words unworthy to preserve.

Dedication and Acknowledgment

I dedicate this book to Ma'am Neneth,
Poetic doctrines taught you me I'll ne'er forget.
You are Anne Sullivan to Helen Keller,
The Mentor for the world's best-seller.
To Brother Chris Orcuse, many thanks and grace,
Although we have not yet met face to face.
  Unfinished could have been my written craft,
  Without your help it'll just remain a draft.

I dedicate this book to hopeless bachelors,
You'll never have to pay for marriage counselors.
I dedicate this book to all Vilmanian fans,
In merriment, let's toast our Sprites in cans.
  And thank you all who bought my previous book,
  Upon completion, many sleepless tears it took.

About the Author and Blurb

Puróy Manalo, the author of the books
"Froilan's, Limited," "Puróy's Second," books that shook
The modern concept modern bards mistook
As poetry— he shook what droopy eyes mislook.
His fourth is in the making, out by May,
The major bookstores briefly will display.
  To be translated in eight tongues across the seas,
  This viral news is like the buzzing of the bees.

Mistake he not as academic nerd,
He wears no glasses, grows no bushy beard.
He wears blue faded jeans and tattered shirts,
And witnessed gory deaths and hopeful births.
  The author is a bagger in some grocers' stores,
  By night, a maker of fine jambs and doors.

Our Next Stop-Over: Planet Earth

We are the minstrels in this sordid land,
We stop to eat, relieve, or see that bank of sand.
Compose your works, or paint, or sing your song,
But do it fast— our Bus will not wait too long.
Do not go farther than the railings, here you'll stand;
Those foreign signs? There is no need to understand.
  Go order there your coffee, mild or strong,
  But promptly ride the bus when you hear the gong.

The Agency demands that you should show result,
And leaving trash behind shall be deemed an insult.
The Chairman wants his money's worth in art,
So do your pieces for the glory of his heart.
  Enjoy the trip with Us, there's nothing wrong,
  You give results, or else you'll be out of the throng.

Puróy Manálo

Thirteenth Month Pay

I'm sorry, Boss, I can't accept that pay
Called thirteenth month, for there is no such month or day.
It is against my firm belief that are just
Twelve months a year, and so decline I must.
I stand for truth, as pure as morning sunshine's rays,
And if I must, unto the dust I'll lay.
  My truthful words are surely you can truly trust,
  We have just twelve months even if the world be dust.

So keep your thirteenth-month, for it's a lie,
I would not settle for a single ply.
Because there are just twelve months in a year,
It's better if you pay me twelve months-worth of beer.
  Unsatisfied was I, for one-twelfth of my pie,
  Give me a dozen pies, or else, goodbye!

Epitaph

Here lies at rest the author's father's bones,
His grave was done in smooth and polished stones.
His father said to him: "I will not see the day
When you'll graduate, make something, I pray,
Out of your self, and be successful in your life;
I hope you multiply— but— find a wife."
  His father's hopeful for a bloomy future,
  But grew up loser as if life's a torture.

O Papa Dear, if you could only see
What I am now and what a future me I'll be.
How difficult my life had been and how
In tears I labored vainly then… but now…
  You should be proud your son is now a man,
  If you were still alive, you could have been my fan.

Seclusión Perpetua

If I were rich, I could have been an old recluse,
And out of town was common poor excuse.
I could have built a marble villa near the falls
Of Malicboy, with subterranean halls;
Amidst the forest, and atop the mountains,
The cool air breezing in so near the fountains.
  A hermit's calm repose in nature's bosom,
  On heights much nearer God, my mind's in blossom.

If I were only wealthy, I could have paid
My doctor, Richard Gere had he me been made.
From Malicboy I'll tacitly buy peace,
Belligerents instead would read my masterpiece.
  I could have purchased beauty, world peace, privacy,
  The world could have respected my celibacy.

On A Single Night

Some decades passed tired waiting for a child,
And then you came one night, with breezes soft and mild.
Much joy you brought us, and hopes of growing old,
A son to care for us when winter nights are cold.
We've witnessed your first steps; I'm the first to trim
Your supple hair; our love did overflow the brim.
  You could have been a teacher or an engineer—
  Had you been adult, varnished you our lives' veneer.

A decade full of love— and full of hope—
Was shattered fast beyond our comprehensions' scope.
Among the innocent souls and angels sing,
That we should have the goodness life can bring.
  My sainted son, be happy up above,
  Five decades more, we'll be united in God's love.

O Calcutta!

O hear this song, Calcutta of the south,
I've written lyrics out of my poetic mouth.
We both have earned our freedom from the West,
So lay we now our common griefs to rest.
We freely read the books and sing the songs,
And freely can we beat the varied gongs.
  Calcutta, free Calcutta, song of Asia,
  Of pink magenta, and of fuchsia.

Of various languages we speak and hear,
A mutual friend, and end, we should not tear.
We sing a common song— the song I've written—
Much softer than the song of a hungry kitten.
  Calcutta, free Calcutta, song of Asia,
  Of pink magenta, and of fuchsia.

God Bless America

Thank God! you gave us rights to worship God,
Our own volitions in a legume pod.
This protein-rich and fibrous conscience
Today may choose between the fraud and innocence.
His Word all seekers freely can avail,
The persecutions now cannot prevail.
  This island paradise is free to choose
    Salvation's house in which their souls they'll never loose.

We praise the same three personed Elohim
Diversity in union, pray we unto Him.
These New World white men gave us godly choice,
Let's listen to their missionary voice.
  In God we trust because America is just,
    Through them He saved these Islands from an empire's lust.

Peace of Mind

The outside world around me resonates with war,
The sudden blasts and fighting echoes far.
(I wonder who is the new President now,
And who's the General to whom the masses bow.)
I pray my childhood friends have crossed the border,
I'll stay behind to nurse the wounds of my brother.
  Most people fear the worst is yet to come,
  Forget they how to pray for Godly calm.

The world is busy, focused with its self,
While leisurely I read my books off the shelf.
Just sipping coffee unhurried, relaxed,
Plain pleased to think that I am now untaxed.
  Just sitting by the fire, my pet Cat on my lap,
  Reciting poems with sounds of distant thunderclaps.

Robert

Now spring is in the air, the Frost has thawed,
Today's young troubadours in envy crawled
Beneath the shadow of a glorious bard—
We don't deserve his invitation card.
That sage named Frost has cast the mould of verse
For us to measure modern works if bad or worse.
  Escuadra of a golden age that waxed and waned,
  We'll have to learn so glory be regained.

By God's will, I'll be the Frost of the East,
I'll raise his genre like a dough with yeast.
If such a dream my pen wouldn't cause me to bring,
Then I should be the third millennium's Bard and king.
  If I should stand below your gilded pedestal,
  Then lucky me with just my silver pall.

My Last Last Will to the Poet's Daughter

Dear Eldest Daughter, Think ye not the candlewax,
But don't forget to pay my cemetery tax.
Or else they'll throw away my barren bones,
And take away my lot for some unsettled loans.
It's just a dollar for every year of stay,
It'll never be a heavy load in any way.
  Beseech ye I, that ye must pay my rent,
  That I in heaven now my time be spent.

Remember, daughter dear: I've paid our taxes full,
And you have studied in the poshest school.
My lot in Pag-ása Island is now yours,
You'll come to see the Chinese cutters sail their course.
  If paying dead men's taxes is a curse,
  Then to the living go to spend your heavy purse.

Tantalus

A dream within my easy reach was lost,
Best efforts my whole life the cost.
My daily outputs— beautiful as daily sunsets—
Not mentioned in domestic TV sets.
Unnoticed in a bookstore thick with dust,
There on a corner shelf among the books of lust.
  My works deserve a better advertisement,
  And not among the perverts' raw enticement.

Display among the masters of this art,
Along the holy, and the scientific smart.
It's not just money nor fame I'm after,
It is 'bout faith, hope, love and laughter.
  See, this is not commercial, just advocacy,
  Nor this political or idiosyncrasy.

My Ex-Face

I saw a photo of a former me,
The scars of recent years I cannot see.
The low and narrow hairline of a decade past,
Reminds me that all glories never last.
Just like the tweeting of the birds I was,
Today of quacking and of breaking glass.
  I wilted like a desiccated rose,
  Unseen like a pimple on your nose.

The glamour of my glorious image
Now past spoiled like a rotten cabbage.
This scrapbook of faded brown and yellow
I'd rather give away to a grateful fellow.
  If girls didn't look at me when I was younger,
  Then getting me a wife will be much tougher.

Coffee Cat

Upon my coffee table lies my Cat,
She loves it shiny, littered, cold and flat.
Among my pen, my coffee cup and book,
My Cat on table top, at it I love to look.
I love my cuddly Cat, I love her so,
She catches little mice, my greatest foe.
  She'll stretch her limbs and yawn contentedly,
  Then she'll attack my coffee heatedly.

O Cat, O Cat, my lovely Cat with pen,
I need my table, find another den.
Now go and find a feline mate to bred,
Of fellow colour, size and creed.
  It will do us no good if you'll just sleep,
  Go down below before the night is deep.

Way Ahead of Schedule

I said last season to expect a little less,
But read the second book and shout, "O yes!"
More poignant than a jellyfish,
Way better than a promise, denser than your wish.
You marveled at my less than a hundred pages,
But now you get a double of your gauges.
  In volume I give for expected quantity,
  Be shocked produced I unexpected quality!

I promised, "...out by May," but look and gasp,
My prompt delivery is hard to grasp.
I give you something better than the first,
The third shall be the best to satisfy your thirst.
  Prepare thy self, the best is printing soon,
  For now the author's busy in his silk cocoon.

Sincerely Yours, Onésimus

Eight poems a week, my father should've been proud,
He'll hear the meek as well one hears the loud.
My father died not knowing what I'll be—
I've spent my life just drinking fancy tea.
But now I'm half his age— his book's middle page—
  I only drink stale water clearer than pale beige.
  My Tátay, could have been so proud of me,
  Had he been living now, my fame he'll see.

He'll see my dozen children with my pretty wife,
And share my blissful and abundant life.
I'll show him my Pulitzers and Nobels,
My plaques, my silver cups and golden bells.
  I bloomed at forty-two, not bad a start,
  If I should live a hundred twenty-six in art.

In the Book Fair

I saw my love as I was signing books,
Disheartened longingness, remorse were in her looks.
She fell in line to have my autograph,
And deep in me I want to loudly laugh.
When 'twas her turn, she handed me the book to sign,
She was drooling like a demented swine.
  I smiled at her and signed the book she bought,
  Regretful smiles she thanked me, so I thought.

Pretended I that I didn't know her, so,
She tearfully turned to sit, she sat too slow.
Now vengeance is mine, and hers repentance,
"Deserve I now respect and your acceptance.
  "You know now what I'm worth so better claim me now,
    Before I give somebody else my marriage vow."

Well Experienced, Now a Poet

I was a Jack of all trades, master to none,
Thanks be to God, I found my niche under the sun.
Cabinet-making destroyed my body,
And cumbersome HR jobs had been so bloody.
I've balanced and consolidated accounts—
The daily stress one such as me surmounts.
  Envérga, many thanks, I'm now an author,
  To thee as payment I will share this honour.

To my mother's hometown, Catanáuàn,
In gratitude, I'll treat you to a *chow fan*.
Your teachers taught me poetry and art,
No longer will I be treated like a fart.
  Thus, many thanks, my God, her town, my school,
  My esteem and pocket learnt to keep our cool.

The Quota and the Deadline

I have to write a little faster than
The constant sun's reliable tan.
For days are shorter now that I am old,
Produce I hotter embers for the cold.
I have to glean by the critical fan—
Winnowing fan— to blow away the chaff and bran.
  I have to mill the daily grind in mind
  Before I leave this worrisome world behind.

If I were only younger when I began,
I could have given honour to my clan.
I have to fill the P.O. and the downtime,
The backlog should be treated in my own time.
  So rush I go to meet my life's demands:
  To satisfy my readers' stern commands.

Renaissance

In a sudden burst of thoughts— a rush of songs—
Among a multitude of varied tongues and throngs.
We all shall sing a common hymn of peace,
And dance together to my musical piece.
Poetic jousts, dance in a poem and book-reading—
More filling than mediocre posts that look trending.
  'Tis nothing new, just a revival movement,
   Requires it only love and the mob's involvement.

A poem a day keeps the psychiatrists away,
Thus poetry's the madhouse you won't have to pay.
The lunatics are those who shun instruction,
They know not that they're dashing to their destruction.
  Let's celebrate a healthy sonnet boom,
  We should not settle for an intellectual gloom.

A Bachelor's Cat

I did the laundry, hung them on my clothesline,
Then ate my rice and fish, dessert's a cloud nine.
I went to work, my Cat at home did stay,
To watch over my rooms while I was away.
The sky was cloudless, the weather should be fine,
My clothes will dry just hanging on the line (?).
  But while at work it rained so suddenly hard—
  I think my feline guard neglected her ward.

That night I came home welcomed by wet shirts and socks—
My kitten's sound asleep in her sleeping box.
I think an animal companion's not enough,
I better find a human mate to do my stuff.
  If I were rich, I'll take a dog, or take a niece,
  Who will look after my home interests in peace.

"I Googled It"

One day they (?) asked me why I know too much,
  I said, "I've 'googled' it!"
    Google, Google, oh keep googling!
Today I researched things about the Golden Touch,
  It said' "Please wait a bit."
    Google, Google, oh keep googling!
All knowledge is now in the global web,
There's no excuse to be an ignorant pleb.

Don't waste your time on shallow posts and tweets,
There's more to get from meats than empty sweets.
I'll pay for wisdom from the Wand'ring Dutch,
  "He'll say, "Just 'google' it!"
    Google, Google, oh keep googling!

    Google, Google, just keep on googling…

The Prototype

Yes Sir, this is a prototype, but soon
The upgrade will be out to take you to the moon.
For just a little more than twenty dollars, you'll
Fly higher than the clouds— that's way too cool (./!)
My best creation's on my study table,
I'll send you finished goods when I am able.
  Please kindly wait, have patience, Doc is cooking,
  The golden quality is in the booking.

Some obsolete conveniences shall stay,
'Til new contraptions seize the changing day.
I'll modify the product to your modern needs,
Until my aging mind no longer bleeds.
  The test drive is worth more than what you'll pay,
  So hold your breath, and keep your cash at bay.

The Prescription

A verse a day, sends the doctor away—
So spread this balm I made from dung and clay;
And take these pills dug out of termite hills,
Your ills will pass away through windowsills.
The doctor's out, and I, the janitor must
Prescribe a quicker cure (that you can trust).
  You have stage seven cancer of the hair,
  You'll die of renal problems on a dental chair.

I see it on your palm that death is near,
But not a relative will shed a tear.
This crystal ball has said it all, that you
Should have been married— options were not few.
  Here comes the Doc from smoking in the lift,
  I have to finish my daily sweeping shift.

Continue to Perpetuity

My name? It might as well be Nameless None,
But please mark all the good I've ever done.
My Saviour cancelled all my debts in full,
So count my deeds that passed the golden rule.
I'll let you imitate my home-made style,
Remember though to walk the extra mile.
  My legacy's a template for improvement,
  Develop it for a literary movement.

A seed can germinate a patient week,
But takes a decade to fill a *pùlanggá*'s beak.
A tree can yearly feed the birds for years,
Before the wood be used to burn our frozen tears.
  I sow the fragile germ on fertile ground,
  Make sure to prune it, be fruitfully heaven-bound.

The Baccalaureate Guest Speaker

A Happy Graduation, students, parents, peers,
I speak now on the podium ... despite your fears.
I thank my Alma Mater for inviting me
To speak in front of you, so nervous I can see.
This won't take long, it'll take a minute (and an hour),
I'll talk until your faces look too sour.
  As an alumnus, I'll declaim my piece,
  For my belovèd school's prized pride and peace.

I studied here with youthful hopes and dreams,
And now I shred illegal prints in reams.
You're fortunate your roster lists my name,
You'll share my infamy and sorry shame.
  Well known am I among the wanted list,
  Applause you must, and that's what I insist.

Aristotle's Oasis

I dreamt that I was walking in the desert,
I saw a stage dressed in a music concert.
Before it lies a fountain filled with coins,
Italian men waded through it— coins up to their loins.
It jets the sweetest wine I've ever tasted,
But overflowing to the desert sand, it's wasted.
  A thousand floodlights filled the starry night,
  This is the kind of jam that feels so right.

We danced, we ate, we sang to Tommy Shaw,
And Simon's ten thousand people there I saw.
The marble fountain misted the night with wine,
Its spray is like mountain fog— so smoothly fine.
  I woke up realizing I forgot my meal,
  The festive dream so vividly seemed real.

A Dozen Roses in the Scrap Bin

I was carpenter who loved a nurse,
I gave my heart but she did not reimburse.
I offered her a bunch of roses— as red
As life itself— but she refused and fled.
I bought those flowers for her and hers alone,
And so I threw it in the bin of the unknown.
  What is the worth of a rose given to a girl
  Who's not your heart's sole precious pearl?

My love is biodegradable waste,
It's all original, not copy paste.
It could have been recycled for some other future use,
Yet she's confused and still my nurse refuse.
  You could have been my wife, you stupid fool—
  Had I been rich, you would not been so cruel.

For My Protégé

A thousand poems— it's such a biblical ambition—
But better start while I can still envision.
By His Grace, and, with patience, I can fill
Demands the worldwide market asks… and quench its thrill.
I'll humble brag for my nephew *Bótchok*'s sake,
My fame (but not my money) he may take.
  I'll never see another century,
  So tell the tale despite the penury.

So what if I go global yet die poor?
At least your uncle's now a famous troubadour.
I took my first step up before the sunset hour—
You'd better do your part before your brain went sour.
  Try being a poet, we're of that stock—
  A Marlowe singing to his nymph and flock.

Maverick

'Why won't you stay in a single place?' you ask,
I have a feral soul, and an aimless task.
No use in dropping anchor on a certain shoal—
I have no steerage over the whims of my soul.
I've no desire to pull my fortune's rein,
It'll only lead to insufferable pain.
  I'd rather wander off on life's vast verdant fields
  Than idly stay in what another man builds.

My earthly home is Earth itself, its crust,
I'll live in a house on wheels if I must.
This planet's wide expanse shall be my bed,
And here you'll bury me when I am dead.
  Don't brand my hide for my spirit is free,
  I'll roam these prairies' breadth— untie me from this tree.

2023 Point 99

Another year is coming with new hopes and dream,
This past year's tears were flowing like a stream.
Frustrations overflowed my patience's banks,
But still I stood against my fortune's pranks.
I kept on bending to the unyielding soil,
In hopes of harvests well beyond my toil.
  I'll go on working 'til there is no other source—
  'Til my fate goads me to an alien course.

Another year is coming with new faith and dream,
I'll get a taste of butter, milk and cream.
If I wouldn't have to lift a finger, still,
I'll labour for my bread, for it's His will.
  I pray this coming year be merciful to me,
  Past sorrows be swallowed by the sea.

The Rush

A writer's piece is like a cavalry charge,
Though most must die that some may make it to the barge.
Incessant barrage is what it takes
To break it through the barricades and stakes.
On bloody ground your poems were piled in a heap,
As if the people thought it lowly cheap.
  Just keep on doing what's have to be done,
  We'll be martyrs for the pen when guns were gone.

They may not know it but the day will come,
When they will sing your song with dolesome drums.
For now be satisfied your books were printed,
Someday your fame on windows will be tinted.
  Have patient faith, but keep on pushing through the line,
  A glorious future shall be yours and mine.

Simplicity

My brazen bracelet was broken by the brackish brook,
So sorry, someone else must search for something I forsook.
Alliteration aside, it's only made
Of bronze and brass, its value will surely fade.
I kept on walking, writing every now and then—
My trinket paled against my poetic pen.
  All superficial ornaments worn by Man,
  Are trash compared to a simple, silent swan.

The plain and simple, naked truth,
Is sweeter than a youth with athlete's foot.
For beauty lies within a childlike heart,
And not on painted faces like a child-made chart.
  No gem nor gold can quench an artist's thirst,
  Our art and Nature's call should be heeded first.

The Future Is A Book

How nice it is to see you children reading,
Than see you watching DIYs 'bout breeding.
In books are wisdom for your future pleasure,
Keep reading them with faith and leisure.
Invest in learning, save knowledge in your mind,
And time will come, a hoard of treasures you shall find.
  A shallow laughter leads to hunger—
  It'll also cause your parents grief and anger.

This book's for you to read and cherish,
 I've written this so you won't perish.
Through books I was taught to fly like Peter Pan:
Indeed, I can fly— in a way— I can.
  You are what you read, therefore, you are,
  A book can lead you high and far.

The Empty Pocket

It's been a long, long time ago since I felt
My pocket heavily pulling down my belt.
My wallet feels so thin and weightless—
It's like a wife caught being faithless.
At times my wallet's full of pawn receipts,
They make me feel I'm trapped in poverty's deceits.
  I hope to see B. Franklins in my purse,
  And not pawn brokers' papers— these worse than a curse.

A lighter burden it is, an empty pocket,
It felt like an eye popped out of its socket.
By now I can walk faster wearing lighter pants—
For now, at least, that's what my spirit wants.
  So light, so light! I fly with wings on my thighs!
  At last, I'm free from avarice's gripping vise.

The Baccalaureate Guest Speaker 2

..That being said, I've been consistent in the list,
Yet not a pair of cuffs have ever bound my wrists.
You might say that I am a braggart when
I say that I'm the most untouchable of men.
D'État? C'est moi! because I pay the best,
The law can't touch me in my lofty nest.
  You see, dear graduates, I've studied well,
  And now I stand alone but others fell.

You see on television how I fared—
You know how they, my enemies, despaired.
An empire I have built to last a thousand years—
I'm richer now despite their widows' tears.
  So study well, dear children, be a younger me,
  And thou shalt see, thy critics hanging on a tree…

Thus, finally…

Poetry

A poem is a multi-personed entity,
A paradox of words in eternity.
At times divine, at times so earthly low;
At times both white as a dove, and black as a crow.
A poem can be dark and bright... or deathly pale;
Or spicy sweet and sour, or bland and stale.
  A poem is art for art's sake— in itself—
  No gem nor gold can give a single bit of help.

A poem can be soft or solid stone;
As graceful as a crane, or rigid as a bone;
As effortless as how an eagle fly,
As purposeful as crows seek where carrions lie.
  A poem is a poem as art is an art,
  Whatever is the purpose, it will do its part.

Thanatopsis

Why be afraid of something that will surely come?
All of us to there must go, the rich and the bum.
Most certain in this world are tax and death—
Taxes can be paid, but you can't buy your breath.
There's nothing owned to pay for life eternal,
Everything's His, whether in- or external.
  Don't fool your self, you cannot save your soul,
  A sinner's death is sure no better than a fowl.

You can't avoid what's coming in the end,
You'll never know when Death's behind the bend.
Of Death's precision, of that we can't pretend—
Let's just accept what fate our God may send.
  Why worry 'bout the end while still alive?
  You'll only let your self from joy deprived.

Time

Don't waste your time, for time is running out,
Once wasted it can never be regained, no doubt.
Make use of it with quality in mind,
In it a treasure trove you'll surely find.
Don't ever waste it on a nonsense goal,
Nor let your life become an empty hole.
  Our precious time is like a falling star,
    You cannot catch it nor keep it in a jar.

Walk your life in a straight line climbing up;
Stop counting the shards of a broken cup.
Unfinished jobs must never see the night,
Complete your work while we still have the light.
  Don't sleep your time away nor walk on aimless ways,
    Fulfill your purpose ere the end of days.

The Future

I wonder what the fourth millennial race might say—
Of what its youth might think of us alive today.
Will they ever know our names and deeds— and misdeeds—
Discover our shame, and our collective greed?
Will they laugh at our jokes, or cry for instead?—
They might as well not understand the words we said.
  A thousand years from now, archaic we shall be—
  A dumb race we have been, the world shall see.

We tried our best to destroy our selves and kin,
We act like being bellicose is not a sin.
If ever this book survived the Apocalypse,
Then let it shine— a sliver of hope past the eclipse.
  The next millennium then shall read
  That we'd been wisely faithful to the pacifists' Creed.

Burning on Both Ends

A candle on both ends— I gripe
That it's the metaphor of my brief life.
I can't afford the luxury of time,
To leisurely enjoy the beauty of a rhyme.
So let me burn 'til both ends meet (♪)—
I ought to do my job despite the wind and sleet.
  I kept on giving light through the window down the winding road—
  That fellows find respite from their tiresome load.

I know my wax was spent on what it's meant,
So I will keep on shining 'til I'm spent.
Pray that another stick shall take my place,
To guide those pilgrims to a warmer grace.
  A younger candle made to burn much longer,
  Is what this world must have, and not warmongers.

Kamag-anak, Inc.

I see it in the applicant's eyes
Some lies that weren't supposed to be there.
Referred to by a client who also told me lies
About the kind of workers that they prefer.
They asked for it, I should comply,
This unqualified girl should pass, no matter why.
  "Forget her Sacks completion test, Purdue,
    For she is hired no matter what you do.

"Attach these in her 201-file, make her start
Tomorrow in my staff, where she is now a part.
Forget psychology, for she's my niece—
For every dozen that I'll have, she'll get a piece.
  All others should be screened and profiled through—
  For pooling— or short-list one pax as cleaning crew.

Híjo de Ferrócaríl

"Chug! Chug!" the *maquinísta* blew the horn
To tell us that I'm going home to where I was born.
I'm leaving Tutubán Station for Malicbóy—
Delightedly my childhood friends will shout: "Puróy!"
My seatmate asked: "*Maúlî, 'Noy?*"
I said: "*Daé*," for Quézon is my joy.
   "*Konduktór, Konduktór*, wake me up in Malicbóy,
   Don't drop me farther off and be Sipócot's toy."

I hope to see once more that leafless *Nárra* tree
Beside the station where I came to be.
And on the railroad tracks, for sure you'll see,
Astride a trolley, a young, happy me.
   Within my yearning heart, a fire still burns
   For frequent happy, sweet returns.

Froilan's Touch

I wish to have King Midas' golden touch of old,
So I can turn these bags of brains, to bags of gold.
What is the use of a heavy head
If hopes of luxuries are dead.
I do not want to be like H. Thoreau,
Who died not reaping profits, but a few.
  For what's the use of a *zacáte* grass?
  The horse had died already, together with an ass.

I need it now while I am still alive,
From me, life's sweetest bounty, don't deprive.
I don't have children to receive my sonnet's sale,
These might as well be like a feather on a scale.
  Dear Readers, help me sell my works and books,
  I have to make a living, sorry as it looks.

Valentine's Day

There are some couples walking by— they're holding hands—
So sweet and happy— this I cannot understand.
It only makes me ask: When will I meet the 'one'?
Or who she might be— my missing half under the sun?
Where is the one to call my own?
I'm tired of waiting all alone.
  "I wonder what'll your name might be—
    Your face is what I want to see."

"Were you already born or should I wait
Another decade 'til I lose my faith?"
"Or are you even human or just a flimsy hope—
A filament beyond reality's scope?"
  "Come now, my 'sole exclusive One and only,'
    Don't let my Valentine's be lonely."

Sóla Grátia

...And I believe in life eternal,
But also, I believe in the damned infernal.
We had the prophets, and we have the preachers,
There's no excuse to ditch the Teacher.
Believe I Calvin's God is like a three-pronged spear,
Who, through the sinews, tendons, bones and flesh, can tear.
  Don't take me for a fool, I know my Book,
  His Word can free you from the devil's hook.

I don't care on which flock you do belong,
As long as you believe that He was never wrong.
By grace, through faith, we shall regain our ties
With Him that were unknotted by the serpent's lies.
  We don't deserve salvation— by our deeds—
  We cannot earn it— 'though the world should bleed.

The Hopeless Alchemist

I built a bridge of paper over life's deep gap,
Only to learn that I had made myself a trap.
A futile effort it had been,
The wide and rushing waters I should've seen.
I tried to cross the paper bridge
In hopes of reaching the summit of that lofty ridge.
  But fragile was my bridge against the hail,
  It tumbled down, and thus, I failed.

No better off was my paper boat,
Above the waters, a few moments did it float.
What I did *on* paper all did fail,
So I might as well just burn my paper trail.
  With all audacity, I must be bold—
  I wish to have King Midas' golden touch of old.

Practicality

At least, I'm free from avarice's gripping vise,
But better yet, I wish I have been worldly wise.
With an artist's heart, and a merchant's mind,
I could have kept a pot of gold that none can find.
It would be better if I just keep on sweeping floors,
Or keep on making cabinets and doors.
  At least, the money there is real and solid,
  Although my clients may be dull and stolid.

It's only practical but plain and true,
That only we, the working class, can construe.
A stack of papers are just pieces of paper
If not sold to feed a poetic pauper.
  The scale is tipping from the pad and pen,
  This hand might wield the hammer once again.

Paper Hopes

This hand might wield the hammer once again,
In the other a chisel, instead of a pen.
Why can't these verses turn into gold?
These unto the devil, I should've sold...
I'll write my way to infamy and shame,
Or saw my self to death without a name.
Undone, Undone! my labours were in vain,
Alas! I drown in an unfathomable pain!
That mountain ridge, this foggy pit...
Ah... from all endeavours I should quit.
There is no gain in writing songs and verse—
I can't eat a paper bread— nor fill a paper purse.
A paper dream it was, my hopeless songs—
Was awakened by the noise of discordant gongs.

On Paper Ground

I was awakened by the noise of discordant gongs,
They rang and echoed through the gorge of songs.
The fjord was hopelessly damp and deep—
Unto the bottom of the chasm, I'd better leap.
The love that I deserve, the honour I should gain,
With wealth and pleasures, were replaced by tears and pain.
  I built my dreams upon a paper ground,
  And all was shattered on a hope unsound.

Why can't these turn into gold or steel?
Or something good that I can feel?
I'll die regretfully poor and single,
At least do let my songs among the classics mingle.
  Despite torrential winds and thunderclaps,
  I built a bridge of paper over life's deep gap.

A Sonnet for You
I need a rhythm that plucks the strings of hearts;
A rhyme that's sweeter than French apple tarts;
Alliteration with the right warmth returning;
A symphony like you that halts my heart from spurning.
But most of all, I need a rhyme for you,
Your name with stem or chem, just can't pass through.
  But yet a softly whispered breeze from me,
  Is amply soothing as a tranquil sea.

For there's no rhyme as suave as thine sweet name,
So I'll just leave this world a lasting fame.
The ages hence shall sing thy name in serenades,
I've written songs for thee that shall not fade.
  What an enduring love I have for thee,
  That thee from all oblivion are forever free!

      Slide The Window Open
Are you the one, Are you the 'One?'
Or should I wait for someone not yet under the sun?
Is it you, Is it you? The love I've been waiting for?
It feels like you— my destiny that I adore.
Our hearts are beating synchronously the same—
Sharing a wordless love aflame.
  So quickly slide the window open wide,
  And I to fluffy velvet clouds shall ride.

Are you the missing half, the fullness of my soul?—
Let our bodies become one— our lives' predestined goal.
My heart and yours are one, a voiceless shout,
A silent scream, an invisible clout.
  Believe me it is us, there's no mistaking it…
  And see our hearts do have a perfect fit.
          What if…
I sincerely wonder, What will you do,
If ever I fell in love with you?
I fear that I may suffer pain,

And all was lost, and all my love's in vain.
I ask sincerely, Will you love me too?
Or all my hopes and dreams cannot come true?
  I wish for us a home of joy and love,
  With wholesome children blest by God above.

I beg thee quick accept my love with glee,
For you can rarely find a man like me.
Allay my doubts and pick my precious shards—
For this mine heart was broken, scared and scarred.
  Afraid am I to cross that busy street,
  Select the heart I laid before your feet.

Too Late

Not much I ask, just water, salt, and bread—
The things that I will never need when dead.
All horses needed grass for it to live,
But grass is of no use when it is time to grieve.
Vast grasslands, endless pastures, plains, and rolling hills,
Are worthless when I succumb to my ills.
  Wide is this graveyard, it used to be my banquet hall,
  You'll sing my dirges— 'tis a wake and not a ball.

No need for downy beds and marble steps—
I need a doctor, and the freedom of the steppes.
No silver spoon, just heaping plates of food—
A starving fame can bring this man no good.
  I shall be leaving soon… to where I'll never eat—
  A time when I'll concede to hope's defeat.

The Last Ditch Stand

Most others strive for glamour, gold, and glory,
But I for life that isn't as sorry.
For what's existence's worth if burdened constantly
By hindrances to dreams that flee so distantly.
An ever-raging strife this life had been—
And insufficiency shall press me light and lean.
  Fix bayonets, or raise the flag of truce—

Dire fate shall win, whichever I may choose.

This is my last— and this shall last—
May it fare better than my past.
With trenches breached, and rivers crossed over,
I might as well have all the gates tossed open.
  Not much I ask, just water, salt, and bread…
  No trifles needed on my slice to spread.

    The Dying Ember
There's no more log to keep this flame aglow,
And I unto the dark, cold night must go.
The fuel to light and warm this lonely room,
Was spent beyond renewal like an empty womb.
I can't just keep on burning wood,
When there is nothing more to burn, to warm my mood.
  My wood was spent, yet I gained nothing good,
  And nothing's left to cook my meagre food.

I can't go on— I was, and I shall be no more—
And wintry is the night beyond this door.
No more, no more! But I shall go once more tonight—
Again in darkness' bosom— hope to see the light.
  Replenish now my victuals ere the dark,
  And let not flames and ember lose their spark.

    Brimming with Affections
I felt that no one understands my pains—
That I am bound for torment's chains.
With little sympathy, or none at all—
No lover's arms to save me from the fall.
It's cold outside— if you'll just let me in—
Embrace me in your warmth… and let my life begin.
  I can't forever live alone,
  Come share these passions I have ever known.

The cottage of your arms, the fireplace of your heart—
To stay within your realm, when can I start?
My world is getting colder by the day,
So shelter me before my daytime turns to gray.
   Barely alive, and yet my love is green,
   My bones are old, and yet my heart is in its teens.

An Incomplete Sigma
My heart's a mirror— you're reflected here—
There is no recess in my heart that is not clear.
Be careful not to break it 'cause it's frangible—
'Though it's really true and tangible.
Don't pick it like a random flower—
A droplet from an autumn shower.
   I'm not a prospect, nor a nameless thing—
   I am your personal bloom in early spring.

Prefer I smaller coffee tables and a saucer,
And glad to read alone my Goethe and my Chaucer.
That brave new world outside is not my own,
It's warmer here, my room— I'm glad to be alone.
   I'll step outside with you, be by my side—
   Without you I'll die out on the plains, wild and wide.

           Unappreciated
I did my best to entertain this mob,
But all the world is just a snob.
I've given all my mind, my heart, and hand,
But felt I lack a poetic magic wand.
They still don't know the value of a book,
For yet my poems are hidden in a nook.
   Alas, I lost all hope of a life at ease!—
   I'll never see my niche in wealth and peace.

For life seems bitter sour until the end,

And destitution is what fate can only lend.
There can be no cherry on the cake,
For there's no cherry, and no dough to bake.
  How can the arts and poetry still thrive,
  If bards and artists barely can survive?

A Glimpse of Paradise
Such a delight it is to visit Window Six,
And see you smile— my troubles then get fixed.
If my days are jigsaw puzzles, then,
You complete my days to the power of ten.
Let's multiply our kind— you solved my y—
Can't find the value of x, no matter how I try.
  Love is the formula for happiness,
  And you, my Dear, erase my loneliness.

No calculator is enough to solve
This quest for love and joy involved.
You are the answer to the question of my heart,
So give solution to this lovelorn part.
  This passion started when you smiled at me,
  So elevate my joy to a divine degree.

The Last Bridge That I Must Cross
The last bridge that I have to cross before the bend,
Is now at sight below the western sky at day's end.
I chose this road not knowing where it leads—
I walked along while scattering my goodwill seeds.
That bridge is yet too far and barely seen,
But farther was the crossroads where I 've been.
  I got this far— there is no looking back—
  My first steps had been rough and black.

What lies beyond the other side of this—
Could it be a vale of sorrows or a shade of bliss?

And what awaits me when I round the curve?—
I hope to find a prize that I deserve.
  I got this far— there is no turning back—
  My first miles had been bleak and black.

Dead End

I will not gamble trudging back to the rear,
That flimsy bridge was gone, I fear.
No turning back to childhood dreams,
And only forward we may go, it seems.
This barren mountain is now my home,
And this shall be my bed and catacomb.
  This giant mound where I used to roam—
  Today my haunt, tomorrow my tomb.

Dear, throw the lifeline towards my way,
Come save me from this place, I pray.
I'd love to live with you, on neither high nor low,
And on a stable ground we'll sow and grow.
  It's not yet over 'til it's done,
  And hand in hand we'll watch the setting sun.

The Mossy Wall

I travelled slow and far and high,
So tired, and hopelessly I walk on by.
The grassy, narrow paths, winding through the woods,
Under the shadows long without any food.
I climbed this mammoth heap of arid rocks,
Only to find a mossy wall of solid blocks.
  I've spent all my strength to move on,
  And on looking down behind... the groove was gone.

I can't go on forever, I must sleep,
I can't go back down the valley deep.
So here I'll rest my listless soul—
But yet, I have to find myself a hole.
  I've gone a long, long way to get here,

I will not gamble trudging back to the rear.

The First Night
This night is ours, do you feel it too?
There's no one here for loving, just us two.
We'll simply love in truth— no lying—
And those who cheat must lie adying.
The cold and moonlit night is ours to keep,
We'll pile up pent-up passions in a massive heap.
  Come let this be the start of happy years—
  There'll be no more uncertainties and tears.

I spent my life just writing broken dirges—
Complete us love songs while the impulse surges.
I've scattered wide the shattered pieces of my heart—
Tonight let's pick up every missing part.
  Come let this be the start of happy cheers—
  There'll be no more uncertainties and fears.

Speechless
How do I say I love you? How do I propose?
I'll say it in a poem, But how can I compose?
My love is as ineffable as a murky stream,
But warm and verdant as a vivid dream.
If only I could paint this throbbing in my chest,
Then you shall see bright rainbows in the west.
  How can I make you see my shy, well-purposed pose?
  I'll sing it in a song… but how can I compose?

It's something that can shake this Earth,
If only words can overwhelm their dearth.
And even if the words were written down,
I end up tactlessly mumbling like a clown.
  I beg of you an echo chamber to my breast,
  That all the questions of the heart may be addressed.

Regaining Glory

I'm going back to where I started work—
I rise again from being a plain dork.
It's been a while since quality and skill
Stopped growing to my goal and will.
But now I woke up from this stasis vigilant—
Prepared to redress my voice that was so sibilant.
  The chance to soar anew to former heights—
  I'll take the risk, from gloom to glowing lights.

I grew new feathers on my wings—
I'm ready now to face all fools and kings.
A raptor always soars to familiar skies,
And I, shall claim my long-lost prize.
  Delayed was it for dusty, clammy years—
  Delay no further, and I'll dry these tears.

Center of My World

Among the crowd, a face stands out,
My only special one, no doubt.
As if there is no other woman in this world,
My frond of verdant love for you unfurled.
Beyond compare, thy beauty glows,
But greater still my love still grows.
  Thou art the fairest of thy lovely kind,
  As if thou art a work of art the Master signed.

You are the only apple in the grove,
The only priceless Gem in a treasure trove.
O what an Artist is the One Who formed you!
A perfect gift for me displayed true.
  To you alone my eyes are truly pleased,
  And all my doubts and pains were greatly eased.

About the Author

Puróy Manálo

Puróy Manálo was a part-time writer, poet and a factory worker in Candelaria, Quezon, Philippines. He was the author of "Froilan's, Ltd." (ISBN: 9789360499259).

The author studied Bachelor of Science in Secondary Education, Major in English, at Manuel S. Enverga University- Catanauan, Quezon.

He is yet unmarried.

www.ingramcontent.com/pod-product-compliance
Lightning Source LLC
LaVergne TN
LVHW041544070526
838199LV00046B/1820